>> **15** minute
abs
workout

Joan Pagano

London, New York, Melbourne, Munich, and Delhi

In memory of my father

Project Editor Hilary Mandleberg
Project Art Editor Ruth Hope
Project Assistant Andrew Roff
Senior Editor Jennifer Latham
Senior Art Editor Susan Downing
Managing Editor Dawn Henderson
Managing Art Editor Christine Keilty
Art Director Peter Luff
Publishing Director Mary-Clare Jerram
Stills Photography Ruth Jenkinson
DTP Designer Sonia Charbonnier
Production Controller Alice Holloway
Production Editor Luca Frassinetti

DVD produced for Dorling Kindersley by
Chrome Productions www.chromeproductions.com
Director Joel Mishcon
Producer Hannah Chandler
DOP Benedict Spence
Camera Benedict Spence, Joe McNally
Production Assistant Irene Maffei
Grip Terry Williams
Gaffer Jonathan Spencer
Music Chad Hobson
Hair and Makeup Victoria Barnes
Voice-over Suzanne Pirret
Voice-over Recording Ben Jones

First published in Great Britian in 2009
by Dorling Kindersley Limited
80 Strand, London WC2R 0RL
Penguin Group (UK)

2 4 6 8 10 9 7 5 3 1

Health warning
All participants in fitness activities must assume the responsibility for their own actions and safety. If you have any health problems or medical conditions, consult with your doctor before undertaking any of the activities set out in this book. The information contained in this book cannot replace sound judgment and good decision making, which can help reduce the risk of injury.

A CIP catalogue record is available from the British Library

ISBN 978-1-4053-3214-9

Printed and bound by Sheck Wah Tong Printing Press Ltd, China

Discover more at
www.dk.com

contents

author foreword

Throughout my career of 21 years in fitness, my clients have shared with me a wide variety of intimate issues regarding their health and wellbeing and, naturally, their appearance, too. In these private conversations, I've learned that they above all want to be healthy and stay in shape. A fit body is a common goal and if I had to name the most challenging area of the body, I would say definitely it is the mid-section. People of all ages – from 15 to 95 years old – have asked me countless questions about how they can reshape the abdominal region. Women rank protruding bellies, expanding waistlines and flabby abs as three top trouble spots. Men want to know how to lose their love handles and sculpt the ultimate six-pack.

It is very rewarding for both my clients and me when they achieve the results that come from following a dedicated, structured exercise routine. The exercises I've chosen for this book target your mid-section from every angle, using a variety of positions to give you the best results, both aesthetically and functionally. As you tighten your waist and tone your tummy with these exercises, you will enjoy other benefits as well. When you strengthen these muscles, you firm up, giving definition to your torso. You also develop core strength, which improves your posture, creates support for the low back and relieves upper-back and neck pain. A strong core provides stamina, stability and power in your everyday activities. You both look and feel better.

Doing the routines as suggested in this book will tone your abs and strengthen your core. To get even better results, supplement these workouts with regular cardio activity. Cardio exercise will enhance your body's sculpting effect by reducing the layer of fat that covers your muscles to reveal a more defined shape underneath. Do at least 30 minutes of cardio activity – such as walking, jogging, stair climbing, cycling or swimming – five days a week. You don't have to do it all at once: you can do it in 10- or 15-minute increments. Just be sure to squeeze it in.

And, of course, take care to eat a healthy diet every day.

Best of luck in your training programme,

Joan Pagano

sweaty**Betty** foreword

I believe in healthy living, having fun, Cornish clotted cream and
cool tracksuits!

Before I opened the first sweatyBetty boutique in London's trendy
Notting Hill I had no major commitments. Outside of my 9 to 5 job
my time was my own and keeping fit and healthy was fun and easy.
Nowadays, with a husband, three kids and a whole chain of
boutiques to look after, I have very little 'me' time!

I'm the first to admit that finding the time to work out can be a
challenge but it's essential if, like me, you need to juggle your work
and home life. So while I'm unlikely to run a marathon, swim the
Channel or climb Everest in the near future, I can certainly do enough
to keep myself looking and feeling good.

We can all find a spare 15 minutes, a few times a week, in the
comfort of our own home to keep our bodies and minds in check.
So I encourage you to get off the sofa and get active, in sweatyBetty
gear of course!

Tamara Hill-Norton

Founder of sweatyBetty
the UK's leading women's activewear retailer

>> **how to use** this book

This book focuses on abdominal exercises to strengthen and firm your torso, flatten your belly and stretch out the muscles for a long, lean line. The step-by-step photographs offer clear instruction for each exercise, while the gatefolds provide an easy reference for each routine.

The accompanying DVD demonstrates all four sequences. As you watch the DVD, page references to the book flash up on the screen. Refer to these for more detailed instruction. In the book, some of the exercises have a starting position, shown in the inset, and the large photographs show the exercise. Annotations give you tips on proper positioning and white dotted-line 'feel-it-here' circles help you focus on specific areas of the body where you should be able to feel the muscle working.

Each 15-minute programme begins with a three-minute warm-up sequence, which gradually builds in intensity. The main workout consists of 10 minutes of exercises that work the core muscles of the abdomen and spine. Stretches are interspersed to lengthen the muscles and provide a restorative moment. The two-minute cool-down at the end of each routine provides a more complete stretch.

The routines are geared to a beginning level of fitness, although Core Challenge requires more strength and skill. If you are new to exercise, gradually build up to this routine. The introductory spreads, FAQs and general information at the end of the book also offer advice for beginners.

Do the routines 3 to 4 times a week. You can do multiple routines in one day, but must allow a day of rest before repeating them. The recovery time is just as important to the development of the muscle as the exertion. For maximum results, do 30 minutes of moderate cardio activity (swimming, walking or cycling) along with your abs routines.

Safety issues

Before you begin any exercise programme, check that it is safe for you. You will find the Physical Activity Readiness Questionnaire (PAR-Q), devised by the Canadian Society for Exercise Physiology on p117. Complete this first, to see if you need to get clearance from your doctor.

core basics at a glance

▲ Warm-up March in place, page 68

▲ Warm-up Step-touch in, page 68

▲ Warm-up Toe-tap out, page 69

▲ Warm-up Twisting knee lift, page 69

▲ Warm-up Hamstring curl, page 70

▲ Floor Twisting roll-back, page 76

▲ Floor Kneeling lift, page 77

▲ Floor Lengthening stretch, page 76

▲ Floor Forearm plank, page 77

Gatefold A quick glance at the gatefold summaries at the end of each section provides a reminder of sequence and proper form.

13 Bridge Return to neutral position and begin with a Pelvic tilt (inset). Then inhale, exhale, and, starting at the base of your spine, peel your back off the floor, one vertebra at a time, until your torso forms a straight line from knees to shoulders. Inhale as you release down, rolling through the curve in your low back. Repeat 5 times.

torso aligned from shoulders to knees

14 Diamond crunch Lie with your knees out to the sides, soles of your feet together, as close to your body as possible. Connect your ribs to your hips, then rest your head in your hands and tighten your abs. Exhale as you lift your shoulder blades (inset). Extend your arms toward your feet, crunching up higher. Return hands behind your head, release down, and repeat 6 times.

crunch higher as you reach

15 Torso twist Return to neutral position, hands behind head, and bring your legs together, knees and feet touching. Reset your abs. Slowly rotate your pelvis to one side, moving your knees halfway to the floor (inset). Inhale, then exhale and crunch up toward the ceiling 10 times. Relax your knees to the floor and rest in a Spinal twist, turning the head in the opposite direction, then repeat to the other side.

feel it here

legs together, knees and feet stacked

knees halfway to floor

16 Reverse crunch Come into 90-90, legs raised with right angles at hips and knees, and arms resting by your sides, palms up (inset). Inhale, then exhale and pull your belly button in toward your spine, drawing your pelvis toward your rib cage, and lifting your hips. Use control to keep from swinging your legs with momentum. Repeat a total of 10 times.

90-90 position

lift hips

annotations provide extra cues, tips and insights

Step-by-step pages The inset photograph on the upper left gives you the starting position for the exercise, where necessary. The large photographs give you the steps required to complete it.

the gatefold shows all the exercises in the programme

▲ Floor
Pelvic tilt, page 71

▲ Floor
Straight leg lowering, page 71

▲ Floor
90-90, page 72

▲ Floor
Alternating kicks, page 72

▲ Floor
Knee drop, page 73

▲ Floor
Spinal twist, page 73

▲ Floor
Double leg lowering, page 74

▲ Floor
Double leg lowering, page 74

▲ Floor
Spiral ab twist, page 75

▲ Floor
Roll-back, page 75

ank plus,

▲ Floor
Child's pose, page 78

▲ Floor
Side plank, page 79

▲ Floor
Side plank with clam, page 79

▲ Floor
Side stretch, page 80

▲ Floor
Wide "V" stretch, page 80

▲ Floor
Seated spinal twist, page 81

▲ Floor
Forward bend, page 81

>> **focus** on the belly

View the paintings and sculptures in any art gallery or museum and what do you notice? Women have bellies – it's a fact of nature. There are many factors influencing the size and shape of your belly, but one thing is certain – a healthy lifestyle has a positive effect in every case.

Genetics determine your physical framework, including where you will carry body fat (apple or pear shape). All healthy people have fat reserves necessary for proper functioning of their bodies. Fat tends to accumulate in specific areas, and your personal genetics dictate where you will carry yours. Visceral fat found deep in the abdomen (apple) increases your risk of heart disease, but responds rapidly to diet and exercise (see FAQs, pp112–113).

Differences between the sexes can also play a role. Women typically have a higher percentage of body fat compared with men. This is designed to store the energy needed to nourish a foetus and then a baby. Structurally, a woman's pelvis is tilted a little more forwards than a man's so that during pregnancy there is less pressure on the organs since some of the baby's weight is carried by the abdominal muscles. This anterior tilt of the pelvis gives the impression that the lower belly is slightly pushed out, creating a 'pot belly'.

Age-related changes occur that affect the shape of our mid-section over time. 'Middle-aged spread' and 'spare tyres' typically occur after child-bearing as we approach the menopausal years. With advancing age, postural changes can cause spinal curves to become more exaggerated and push the belly forwards.

Many other factors may come into play. Weight gain and stress both influence the size of the belly; repeated pregnancies can affect muscle and skin tone; abdominal surgery can cause a loss of

> ## >> **exercise for** a smaller belly
>
> - **If your abs are toned** but have a layer of belly fat over them, add 30 minutes of cardio most days of the week to burn calories and reduce fat.
>
> - **If you do not have excess belly fat,** but lack of muscle tone causes your belly to hang, you should concentrate on the abs routines to firm up.
>
> - **If you are both** lacking muscle tone and carrying excess fat, step up both cardio (as above) and abs routines. Begin with the Crunch routine.

muscle strength, scar tissue and an accumulation of fluids. Exercise can help improve many of these.

Before you begin, it is helpful to assess your individual issues and focus on the changes that you can make. Then establish a starting point for your programme (see Crunch Assessment, pp14–15, Deep Abs Assessment, pp16–17 and Risk Assessment, pp116–117). Set realistic goals and measure your progress periodically.

So many factors influence the size and shape of your belly, including genetic predisposition, age and lifestyle habits (physical activity and diet).

>> **the anatomy** of your abs

The core region of the body is very complex and technically consists of the collective muscles that control your trunk. The abdominals are central to the core region and work in concert with the erector spinae muscles of the spine to provide stability to the torso.

The abdominals consist of four muscle groups – the rectus abdominis, the internal and external obliques and the transversus abdominis. They are layered, overlapping and connected to each other. They run vertically, diagonally and horizontally and often function synergistically.

The rectus abdominis is best known as the coveted 'six-pack' muscle, which describes the

THE CORE MUSCLES

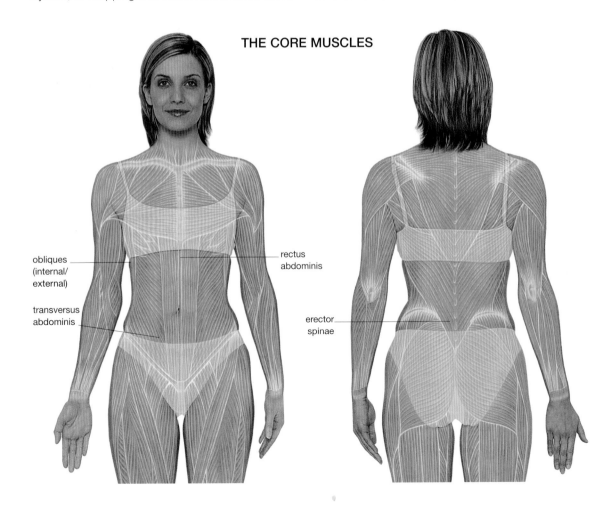

obliques
(internal/
external)

transversus
abdominis

rectus
abdominis

erector
spinae

sections that develop when this muscle is toned. It is the most superficial muscle of the abdomen, running vertically from the sternum to the pubic bone. It functions to flex the spine and stabilize the pelvis as you walk.

The internal/external obliques are found on the sides of the core area and perform multiple functions. When they contract on one side of the body they rotate the trunk (as in the Side crunch, p25) and laterally flex the body (as in the Side plank, p79). When they contract on both sides of the body simultaneously, they assist in flexing the spine and compressing the abdomen (as in the Pelvic tilt, p23).

When it is toned, the transversus abdominis acts as a natural girdle, flattening the abdomen and supporting the low back. It runs horizontally around your mid-section and is the deepest abdominal muscle. This muscle works with the internal/external obliques to stabilize the pelvis in neutral position, as in the 90–90 exercise (p72).

The erector spinae – the spinal extensors – run the length of the spine. Back extensions trigger this group (as in the Back extension using the beach ball, p55), strengthening the muscles for greater trunk support. In plank positions (p99), the erector spinae function with the abdominals to stabilize the torso in the horizontal position.

Like any muscle group, the core muscles require 24 to 48 hours' recovery time between workouts. Although they are primarily endurance muscles, which recover quickly from an abundance of work, they still need time to rest, recover and rebuild. The result will be added strength.

TARGETING CORE MUSCLES

Do your Abs workouts 3 to 4 times a week on nonconsecutive days. Each routine gives you a balanced workout for the abs and spinal muscles. You can do multiple workouts on any given day, but must allow a day of rest before repeating them. The table below shows you which specific muscles are worked by each exercise.

CRUNCH	BEACH BALL	CORE BASICS	CORE CHALLENGE
Rectus abdominis	**Rectus abdominis**	**Rectus abdominis**	**Rectus abdominis**
Short crunch	Roll-back & lift	Roll-back	Double crunch
Neutral crunch	Pullover crunch		Crunch & extend
Long crunch	Reverse crunch combo	**Transversus abdominis**	Kneeling crunch
Diamond crunch		Pelvic tilt	
Reverse crunch	**Transversus abdominis**	Straight-leg lowering	**Transversus abdominis**
90–90 crunch	Reverse crunch combo	90–90	Tuck & roll
Crunch & dip	Toe tap	Alternating kicks	Crunch & extend
Bicycle	Ball transfer	Double-leg lowering	Dead bug
			Toe dip
Transversus abdominis	**Obliques**	**Obliques**	
Pelvic tilt	Side twist	Knee drop	**Obliques**
Crunch & dip	Side reach	Spiral ab twist	Tuck & roll
	Trunk twist	Twisting roll-back	Kneeling twist
Obliques	Balancing side crunch	Side plank	Kneeling crunch
Side crunch			Twisting side plank
Torso twist	**Erector spinae**	**Erector spinae**	Balance & crunch
Bicycle	Forearm plank	Kneeling lift	
	Back extension	Forearm plank	**Erector spinae**
Erector spinae			Kneeling crunch
Arm & leg lift			Plank with leg lift
Press-up			Lat push

>> **crunch** assessment

The crunch is the classic abs exercise, targeting the rectus abdominis muscle that runs from the sternum to the pubic bone. It is a versatile exercise, suitable for beginners or more advanced exercisers. It also ranks as one of the most effective for strengthening the abdomen.

The function of the rectus muscle is to flex the spine, and in the crunch you do not perform more than 30° of spinal flexion (which refers to how high you lift your upper torso off the floor), even if you can raise your torso higher. This range of motion isolates the muscle, keeping the work in the rectus. If you lift higher, as in a full sit-up, for example, you activate other muscles, primarily the hip flexors in the front of the thigh. In addition to being a more effective isolation exercise than the full sit-up, the crunch places less stress on the low back and is therefore safer.

It is useful to have an objective measure of your starting level of abdominal fitness. Together with your health and medical information, a fitness assessment helps define your goals in an exercise programme. Establishing a baseline also enables you to measure your improvement. One way to measure muscular fitness is to count how many repetitions you can perform. Do the crunch test as described below. Write down your results, make a note of the date, and after two months of training, repeat the assessment.

To get the most from your workout, use proper form and execution of the crunch. Concentrate on perfecting the technique and apply it to each repetition. Mental focus also enhances the outcome – think about feeling the abdominal muscle tightening, strength coming from the core centre, lifting from the chest, head relaxed in your hands.

Preparation for the crunch

Make a cradle for your head by spreading your fingertips and supporting the base of your skull (see p15, top right). Bend your fingers slightly and let the weight of your head rest in your hands. Keep your chin lifted, as if you were holding an orange under it (measure the distance with your fist, as in the photograph on p15, top left). Keep your elbows wide to reduce any tendency to pull on your neck.

With your low back relaxed in neutral alignment, engage the rectus abdominis by tightening the connection between the ribs and the hips. Keep tension in the muscle as you lift your chest to the ceiling, shoulder blades clearing the floor. Maintain the tension as you lower your shoulder blades to

Neutral crunch
Count how many neutral crunches you can do consecutively without resting. Remember, this is not a full sit-up. Lift your shoulders no higher than 30° off the mat.

Your score

Excellent	50 or more
Good	35–49 reps
Fair	20–34 reps
Poor	fewer than 20 reps

Fist under chin Use your fist under your chin to gauge the correct alignment of the head. Always think, 'Chin up'.

Position of hands on head Spread your fingers at the base of your skull to create a cradle for holding your head. Remember to relax your neck in your hands.

the floor and, without resting at the bottom, immediately repeat the lift. Keep drawing the ribs to the pelvis – think of 'scooping' out the abdomen. Learn to breathe while you are drawing in, holding tension in the muscle – inhale first, then exhale as you lift up. Use slow, controlled movements and work the entire range of motion. It's quality not quantity that counts!

The weight of your head and upper torso provide resistance in the crunch. You can increase the intensity by

slowing the action, adding holds (as in the Long crunch, p24 and the Diamond crunch, p26), or by adding external resistance. In the Beach Ball workout, for instance, a simple unweighted ball will do just fine; but you can increase the resistance for muscle strengthening by using a weighted ball of 1.4–1.8kg (3–4 pounds) – my favourite are filled with gel. Although there are heavier balls available, it is better to use one of this weight and maintain proper form, being careful not to use momentum in the movements.

Connecting ribs to hips Set your abs before you move. Think of connecting the ribs to the hips. Maintain this connection, drawing ribs to pelvis, while you perform crunches.

15

>> **deep abs** assessment

The deepest abdominal, the transversus abdominis, is a flat, horizontal band of muscle that encircles the waist from front to back. Toning it creates a natural corset-like effect of narrowing the waist, flattening the abdomen and supporting the low back.

The transversus abdominis plays a significant role in core strength. It functions to stabilize the pelvis and maintain the small curve in the low back, which affects your posture and alignment in all positions against gravity, whether you are stationary or moving. In fitness training, sports activities and everyday life, a stable core provides stability for the trunk, which increases the control of the movement you are performing.

A few simple exercises can help you to develop body awareness of your deep abdominals. Belly breathing is key here because the transversus abdominis functions (together with the obliques) to compress the abdomen when you exhale. Practise a belly breath; inhale, fill the belly with air, then exhale forcefully by pulling the abdominals tight (think 'belly button to spine'), then push the air out.

Next, find your own neutral spine alignment, the place where your spine rests while preserving all its natural curves. You should have a slight curve in the low back – with just enough space to slip your hand in if you are standing straight with your back against a wall. It may be more difficult to establish the neutral position when lying down, but it is halfway between a full arch and a flat-back position. The correct alignment of the low back, neither flattened nor arched, will allow you to recruit your core muscles most effectively.

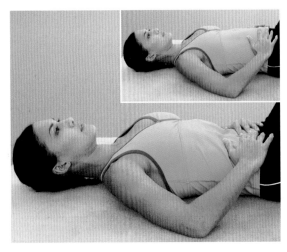

Belly breaths Place your hands on your belly to feel the action of the abdominals as they expand to take the air in (inset) and compress to push the air out.

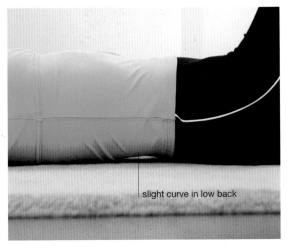

slight curve in low back

'Neutral spine alignment' refers to the resting position of the spine with all its natural curves in place. The low back retains its slight curve and is neither arched nor flattened.

>> tips for **core training**

- **Warm up the pelvis** Do 10 Pelvic tilts with belly breaths to rehearse the breathing, practise abdominal compression and move the pelvis in a controlled way.

- **Active stabilization** Do a strong Pelvic tilt and release halfway, keeping the abdominals engaged, low back relaxed. With the pelvis stabilized like this, breathe naturally.

- **Monitor the position of the pelvis** Place your fingers under your sacrum to make sure it stays level.

The Pelvic tilt can be used as a technique to learn how to actively stabilize the pelvis in neutral spine alignment. Do a Pelvic tilt (see p23) combining a belly breath with a slight rotation of the pelvis – inhale, expand the belly as you take in the air; exhale, compress the abdomen and press the low back to the floor. Now, keep your abdominals tight and release the Pelvic tilt halfway. Relax the low back, allowing the slight natural curve. The abdominals should remain taut or stiff to the touch.

To assess the strength of the transversus abdominis, we challenge its ability to stabilize the pelvis against the changing resistance of various leg movements. There are three levels of difficulty, as shown on the right. All variations are performed lying on your back, with your arms resting to the sides, palms up, to minimize any assistance from the upper body. As you add the leg movements, use your abs to keep your low back from arching and your hips from rocking side to side. A good way to monitor how you are doing is to place your fingers under your pelvis and feel the two bumps on either side of your sacrum just below your waist. As you raise and lower your legs, make sure that the pelvis stays level, exerting even pressure on your fingers, and doesn't lift up on either side.

Assessing the strength of the **transversus abdominis**

Beginner level Engage the abs, lift one leg at a time, keeping the right angle at the knee, then lower the leg back to the floor. Alternate sides for 10 reps.

Intermediate level Come into 90–90, one leg at a time, right angles at hips and knees, low back in neutral alignment. Hold this position for 30 seconds or more.

Advanced level From 90–90, straighten both legs to the ceiling and lower them towards the floor, as far as you can without arching the low back.

15 minute

crunch routine >>

Shape up with the classic crunch, one of the most effective abs exercises

>> **warm-up** march in place/step-touch in

1 **March in place** With feet parallel, knees soft, arms by your sides, begin marching. Add the arms, lifting them up, then back down. Turn your palms up on the lift, down on the release. March for 16 reps (1 rep = both sides).

2 **Step-touch in** Step one leg to the side, arms by your sides. Step the other leg in, touching your feet together, bending your elbows to that side and swinging your hands to shoulder height. Repeat, moving from side to side, for 8 reps.

turn palms down as you lower arms

keep knee low

bend elbows, fists to shoulder height

shift weight from side to side

3 **Toe-tap out** Step your feet apart, arms by your sides. Swing both arms to one side at shoulder height, coming up on the toes of the opposite foot. Circle your arms down to the other side and reach out with the tapping leg. Repeat, alternating sides for 8 reps.

4 **Twisting knee lift** With legs apart, raise the arms sideways to shoulder height. Bend your elbows to 90°, palms forwards. Keeping the back straight, bend one knee to hip height. Rotate your torso, bringing the opposite elbow towards the raised knee. Repeat, alternating sides for 8 reps.

arms swing like a pendulum

reach tapping leg to the side

hold torso upright

lift knee to hip height

>> **warm-up** hamstring curl/body sway

5 **Hamstring curl**
With your legs wider, reach your arms to the sides at shoulder level, palms down. Bend one knee behind and reach for your foot with the opposite hand, raising the other arm up on a diagonal. Repeat, alternating sides for 8 reps.

stretch the fingers

reach hand to foot

6 **Body sway** With legs apart and arms raised, step one leg in, flexing at the waist and head centred between your arms. Repeat, alternating sides for 8 reps.

keep shoulder blades down

torso and head move as one

Repeat Steps 5–1 (reverse order) to complete your warm-up.

spine in neutral

7 **Pelvic tilt** Lie on your back in neutral position with knees bent at 90°, feet flat on the floor and arms by your sides, palms up. Inhale, fill your belly with air (inset). Then exhale forcefully, pulling your abdominals in tight and, with one fluid motion, flatten your low back to the floor. Hold for a moment, then release and repeat 10 times.

knees bent at 90°

pull abs tight

arms resting, palms up

8 **Short crunch** From neutral position, move your feet in close to your buttocks, connect the ribs to the hips, then place your hands behind your head (inset). Inhale first, then exhale, scooping out your abdomen, belly button to spine, as you lift your shoulder blades 30° off the floor. Release, slowly lowering your shoulders (but not your head) to the floor. Repeat 10 times.

keep chin lifted

feel it here

heels close to buttocks

>> **floor** neutral crunch/long crunch

9 **Neutral crunch** Move your feet forwards to neutral position. Tighten your abdomen by drawing your ribs towards your pelvis. Pick up the pace and continue to lift and lower your shoulders rhythmically, exhaling as you lift and inhaling as you release, maintaining tension in your abs throughout the movement. Repeat 10 times.

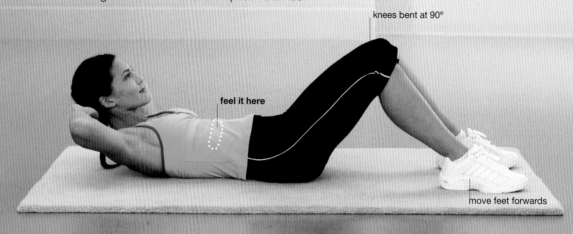

knees bent at 90°

feel it here

move feet forwards

10 **Long crunch** Extend your legs, keeping a slight bend in your knees. Inhale first, then exhale and pull *in* when you crunch *up*. Add a hold at the top of the movement and release slowly. Learn to keep tension in the muscle while you continue to breathe. Repeat 10 times, then stretch out, arms and legs long.

slight bend at the knees

feel it here

move feet forwards

>> crunch

11 **Side crunch** From neutral position, cross one ankle over the opposite knee, hands behind your head (inset). With elbows wide, inhale, then exhale and twist one shoulder towards the opposite knee. Pause, then slowly release without resting your head on the floor. Repeat 5 times on each side.

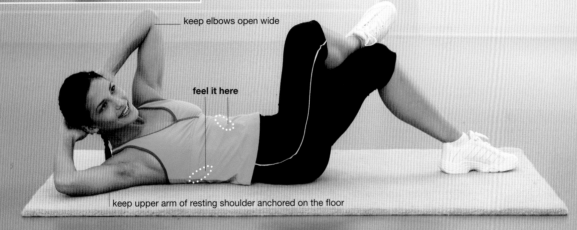

keep elbows open wide

feel it here

keep upper arm of resting shoulder anchored on the floor

12 **Lengthening stretch** Reach out long, extending your arms and legs. Take a deep breath in and stretch out as far as you can. Cross one ankle over the other and take the wrist on the same side in your other hand. Pull to the opposite side, stretching out the entire side of your torso. Pause, then change sides and repeat.

anchor shoulder blades

13 **Bridge** Return to neutral position and begin with a Pelvic tilt (inset). Then inhale, exhale and, starting at the base of your spine, peel your back off the floor, one vertebra at a time, until your torso forms a straight line from knees to shoulders. Inhale as you release down, rolling through the curve in your low back. Repeat 5 times.

torso aligned from shoulders to knees

14 **Diamond crunch** Lie with your knees out to the sides, soles of your feet together, as close to your body as possible. Connect your ribs to your hips, then rest your head in your hands and tighten your abs. Exhale as you lift your shoulder blades (inset). Extend your arms towards your feet, crunching up higher. Return hands behind your head, release down and repeat 6 times.

crunch higher as you reach

Torso twist Return to neutral position, hands behind head, and bring your legs together, knees and feet touching. Reset your abs. Slowly rotate your pelvis to one side, moving your knees halfway to the floor (inset). Inhale, then exhale and crunch up towards the ceiling 10 times. Relax your knees to the floor and rest in a Spinal twist (see p48), turning the head in the opposite direction, then repeat to the other side.

feel it here

legs together, knees and feet stacked

knees halfway to floor

90–90 position

Reverse crunch Come into 90–90, legs raised with right angles at hips and knees and arms resting by your sides, palms up (inset). Inhale, then exhale and pull your belly button in towards your spine, drawing your pelvis towards your rib cage and lifting your hips. Use control to avoid swinging your legs with momentum. Repeat a total of 10 times.

lift hips

>> **floor** 90–90 crunch/crunch & dip

17 **90–90 crunch** Still in 90–90, place your hands behind your head and tighten the connection between your ribs and your hips (inset). Exhale as you lift your shoulder blades, eyes on the ceiling, chin lifted. Repeat 10 times. When you have finished, hug your knees into your chest and rest.

legs stable at 90–90

shoulder blades clear the floor

18 **Crunch & dip** Resume 90–90 with your hands behind your head, exhale and do an upper torso crunch (inset). Hold it while you inhale and dip your toes to the mat. Exhale and return legs to 90–90, then inhale and release the crunch. Repeat 10 times, then hug your knees into your chest for a breather.

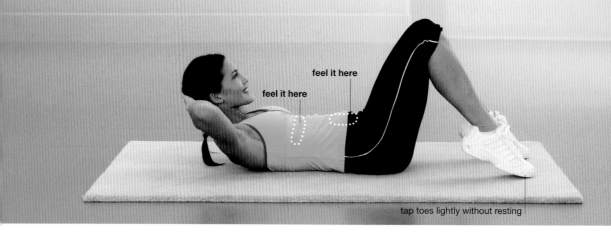

feel it here

feel it here

tap toes lightly without resting

19 **Bicycle** Return to 90–90, hands behind your head. Start with an upper torso crunch (inset), then exhale as you twist one elbow to the opposite knee, bringing your knee into your chest and extending your other leg towards the floor. Inhale back to centre and go to the other side. Alternate sides for 5 reps, keeping your shoulder blades lifted. Reach out long to stretch.

twist shoulder to knee

feel it here

feel it here

20 **Arm & leg lift** Lying face down, extend your arms, palms down. Scoop out your abdomen and press your pubic bone into the floor (inset). With your forehead still resting, exhale and lift one arm and the opposite leg, lengthening the limbs as you lift up. Repeat for 5 reps.

lengthen as you lift

feel it here

fully extend arm

>> **floor** press-up/sphinx

21 **Press-up** Lie face down, arms bent in the shape of a 'W', forearms resting on the floor, palms down (inset). Squeeze your shoulder blades down and together. Lengthen through your torso, reaching the top of your head forwards. Exhale as you lift your head and shoulders off the floor without using any strength from your arms. Keep your nose down. Repeat 8 times.

head and neck aligned with spine

anchor shoulder blades

22 **Sphinx** Lying face down, elbows bent with forearms resting on the mat, anchor your shoulder blades as you lift your chest, sliding your elbows forwards to be directly under your shoulders. Pull your ribs away from your hips, stretching your abdomen (inset). With your shoulders square to the front, turn your head to one side and hold; then to the other.

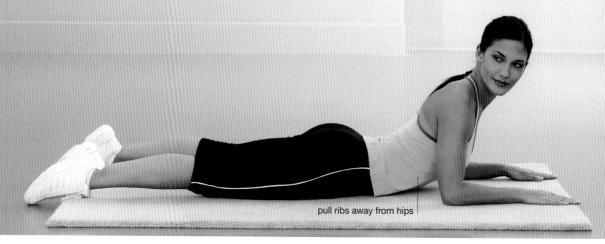

pull ribs away from hips

23 **Child's pose** Sit back on your heels and bend forwards, forehead reaching to mat, arms stretching centre (inset). Walk your hands to one side, keeping your head centred between your elbows, then to the other side. Use your breath to deepen the stretch: let your body sink into the position with every exhale.

head centred between elbows

24 **Spinal curve** Kneel on all fours, wrists under shoulders, knees under hips (inset). From neutral, lift your head and hips up, curving your spine into a 'C'.

lift hips up

lift head up

25 **Spinal arch** Now arch your spine, rounding your back up to the ceiling by tucking your hips under and dropping your head between your arms. Repeat each curve and arch 4 times, breathing naturally throughout.

tuck hips under

drop head between arms

26 **Ear tilt** Sit up tall, hips firmly planted on the floor, legs crossed comfortably in front. Anchor your shoulder blades. Tilt your ear to your shoulder, using your hand on the side of your head to gently deepen the stretch, while you reach down with your other hand to create a dynamic opposition. Hold and breathe.

tilt ear to shoulder

reach down with opposite hand

pull top of head down

27 **Chin tilt** From the previous position, turn your chin to your armpit and place your hand on the crown of your head using gentle downward pressure. Feel a slight shift in the muscles being targeted, now in the back of your neck and upper back. Hold, breathe and then switch sides, repeating both stretches.

turn chin to armpit

roll shoulders backwards

28 **Shoulder roll** Initiate the movement from your shoulder blades. First shrug them up towards your ears (inset), then roll them back and together. Then separate the blades as your shoulders come forwards and repeat once more. Rolling your shoulders backwards will leave your chest open.

▲ **Floor** Pelvic tilt, page 23

▲ **Warm-up** Hamstring curl, page 22

▲ **Warm-up** Body sway, page 22

▲ **Floor** Short crunch, page 23

▲ **Floor** Press-up, page 30

eg lift, page 29

▲ **Floor** Sphinx, page 30

crunch at a glance

▲ **Warm-up** March in place, page 20

▲ **Warm-up** Step-touch in, page 20

▲ **Warm-up** Toe-tap out, page 21

▲ **Warm-up** Twisting knee lift, page 21

▲ **Floor** 90–90 crunch, page 28

▲ **Floor** Bicycle, page 29

▲ **Floor** Crunch & dip, page 28

▲ **Floor** Arm &

crunch >>

15 minute **summary**

▲ Floor
Bridge,
page 26

▲ Floor Diamond crunch, page 26

▲ Floor
Torso twist,
page 27

▲ Floor Reverse crunch, page 27

▲ Floor Chin tilt,
page 33

▲ Floor Shoulder roll, page 33

▲ **Floor**
Neutral
crunch,
page 24

▲ **Floor** Long crunch, page 24

▲ **Floor**
Side crunch,
page 25

▲ **Floor** Lengthening stretch, page 25

▲ **Floor** Child's
pose, page 31

▲ **Floor** Spinal curve, page 31

▲ **Floor**
Spinal arch, page 32

▲ **Floor** Ear tilt

>> crunch FAQs

Proper form and technique are essential to performing a classic crunch. To get the most out of each one, learn the correct form and use it with every repetition. Concentrate on your breathing, alignment and pacing. Focus on keeping your abdomen taut and your ribs connected to your hips throughout the entire set.

>> **I can't get the breathing right. How do you know when to inhale and exhale?**

In all resistance exercises, you exhale on the exertion or when you lift the weight against gravity. In crunches, this is when you lift your upper body off the floor. Think, 'Inhale first, then exhale and move'. If you are a beginner and can't yet keep everything in mind, just remember to breathe. Once you've learned the form, you can focus on the breathing.

>> **My belly pops out when I do a crunch. How can I learn to 'scoop'?**

Practise doing Roll-backs (p75) first. It is easier to 'scoop' the abdomen in a seated position than when you are lifting your upper body off the floor. Next, practise 'belly breaths' on the floor – inhale, fill the belly with air; exhale forcefully, pulling the abs tight. Now apply the same breathing pattern to crunches, drawing the abdomen in as you lift your shoulder blades up.

>> **Should I press my low back to the floor?**

When you lift your shoulder blades or hips in an abdominal exercise, it's normal to feel your low back connect to the floor, but you shouldn't purposely press your back down. The back should remain in 'neutral spine alignment', with the small, natural curve in the low back.

>> I'm feeling strain in my neck. Do you have any suggestions to help?

Before you move, create a band of support in the abdomen by connecting the ribs and the hips. Cradle your head in your hands, chin up. Mentally and physically relax the neck. Concentrate on feeling the strength from your core centre as you lift your chest off the floor. Your head should rest in your hands and remain aligned with your spine.

>> Isn't it better to do a full sit-up than a crunch?

The crunch isolates the abdominal muscles more effectively than a full sit-up, which also activates the hip flexors in the front of the thigh as you come to a sitting position. In the crunch, limit the range of motion to 30° of spinal flexion (even if you can come up higher) in order to keep the work in the abdominals. The crunch is also a safer alternative if you have tight hip flexors and/or low-back pain. A sit-up can exacerbate both of these conditions.

>> My friend does hundreds of crunches every day. How many should I be doing?

Quality is more important than quantity. Two or three sets of 20 reps is enough to condition the abs. The routines in this book vary the exercises to target the same muscle from different positions, instead of repeating sets. This style of training provides additional stimulation to the muscles as opposed to performing multiple repetitions of the same exercise.

>> If I work quickly, I can do more crunches in less time. Isn't this better?

No. The most effective way to get results is to do the exercises more slowly, with controlled form. You need to work the muscles through their full range of motion. Working quickly in a shallow range of motion does not fully develop the muscle. The exercises should be paced according to the instructions and performed with concentration.

15 minute

beach ball
routine >>

The ball adds fun and resistance, giving new energy to traditional exercises

1 **March in place** With feet parallel, knees soft and arms by your sides, begin marching. Add the arms, lifting them up, with palms up, then down, with palms down. March for 16 reps (1 rep = both sides).

2 **Step-touch in** Step one leg to the side, arms by your sides. Step the other leg in, touching your feet together, bending your elbows to that side and swinging your hands to shoulder height. Repeat, moving from side to side, for 8 reps.

turn palms down as you lower arms

keep knee low

bend elbows, fists to shoulder height

shift weight from side to side

3 **Toe-tap out** Step your feet apart, arms by your sides. Swing both arms to one side at shoulder height, coming up on the toes of the opposite foot. Circle your arms down to the other side and reach out with the tapping leg. Repeat, alternating sides for 8 reps.

4 **Twisting knee lift** With legs apart, raise the arms sideways, to shoulder height. Bend your elbows to 90°, palms forwards. With a straight back, bend one knee to hip height. Rotate your torso, bringing the opposite elbow towards the raised knee. Repeat, alternating sides for 8 reps.

arms swing like a pendulum

reach tapping leg to the side

hold torso upright

lift knee to hip height

>> **warm-up** hamstring curl/body sway

5 **Hamstring curl**
Take your legs wider and reach your arms out to the sides at shoulder level, palms down. Bend one knee behind and reach for your foot with the opposite hand, raising the other arm up on a diagonal. Repeat, alternating sides for 8 reps.

6 **Body sway** With legs apart and arms raised, step one leg in and flex at the waist. Keep your head centred between your arms. Repeat, alternating sides for a total of 8 reps.

stretch the fingers

torso and head move as one

keep shoulder blades down

reach hand to foot

Repeat Steps 5–1 (reverse order) to complete your warm-up.

7a **Roll-back & lift** Sit tall, knees bent at 90°, hip-width apart, feet flat on the mat. Hold the ball in front of your chest, arms extended. With your spine straight, pull your torso as close to your thighs as you can (inset). Inhale, then exhale as you roll back, drawing your ribs to your hips and curling your pelvis under. Think of curving your spine into a 'C'.

draw ribs to hips

curve the spine, pull abs tight

7b Hold the position as you lift the ball overhead, then lower it and realign your spine to straighten up. Repeat 10 times.

keep shoulder blades down as you lift ball up

>> **floor** side twist/spinal twist

8 **Side twist** Sit up with your knees bent at 90°, feet relaxed. Hold the ball close to your body, elbows bent. Lean back with your spine straight, chest lifted (inset). Rotate your torso to one side and touch the ball to the floor. Then pause at centre before repeating to the other side. Repeat for 10 reps.

keep back straight

touch ball to floor

9 **Spinal twist** Roll down to the floor, keeping your knees bent and set the ball aside. Stretch your arms out at shoulder level, with your palms facing up and rotate your knees to one side in a Spinal twist. Turn your head the opposite way. Hold for a moment, then change sides.

turn head away from knees

knees and feet stacked

stretch arms out, palms up

spine in neutral

Pullover crunch Lie on your back in neutral position, knees bent at 90° and feet flat on the floor. Hold the ball diagonally overhead with your shoulder blades anchored (inset). Inhale, then exhale, keep your abs tight and lift your torso, reaching the ball to your knees. Release back without resting and repeat 10 times. Then rest and rock your head from side to side.

10

chin up, head and neck aligned

Side reach Lie on your back in the neutral position. Hold the ball towards your knees, arms straight (inset). Inhale, then exhale and lift your shoulder blades, reaching the ball to one side. Hold. Pass through centre to the other side. Repeat for 8 reps, alternating sides. Finally, extend your legs and reach your arms long, with the ball behind your head. Rock your head from side to side to ease any tension in the neck.

11

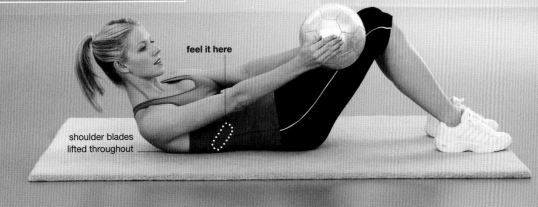

feel it here

shoulder blades lifted throughout

>> **floor** reverse crunch combo

spine in neutral

12a **Reverse crunch combo** Place the ball between your knees and come into neutral position, arms by your sides, palms up (inset). To initiate the Bridge, perform a Pelvic tilt (see p23).

knees bent at 90°

draw abs tight

arms resting, palms up

12b Complete the Bridge by lifting your hips until they form a straight line connecting your knees to your shoulders. Release, rolling down sequentially through your spine.

straight line from shoulder to knee

90–90 position

do a Pelvic tilt as you lift hips up

shoulder blades anchored to keep shoulders open

12c Then immediately initiate the Reverse crunch by raising your legs to 90–90, knees over hips, calves parallel to the floor (inset). Repeat the Pelvic tilt, compressing your abdomen and lifting your hips off the floor in a slow, controlled movement. Continue, alternating the Bridge and Reverse crunch for 8 reps (1 rep = Bridge/ Reverse crunch).

rotate pelvis

knees and feet stacked

knees halfway to the floor

13 **Trunk twist** From neutral position, bring your legs together, knees and ankles touching. Hold the ball to the ceiling over your chest (inset). Lower your knees to one side while you reach the ball to the other. Keep your knees and feet stacked as you rotate your pelvis. Repeat for 8 reps, alternating sides. Now set the ball down and do a Spinal twist (see Step 9) to each side.

>> **floor** toe tap/ball transfer

14 **Toe tap** Hold the ball above your chest, arms straight and take the legs to 90–90. Contract your abs to bring your spine into neutral (inset). Inhale, lowering the ball behind your head as you lower one leg to the floor, maintaining the right angle at the knee. Tap your toes lightly without resting and exhale to return to the start. Alternate sides for 6 reps.

maintain right angle at knees

feel it here

spine in neutral

tap down without resting

15a **Ball transfer** In neutral position, hold the ball behind your head, shoulder blades down. Engage your abdominals to stabilize your upper pelvis against the floor (inset). Inhale first, then keeping your head and shoulders on the floor, exhale and raise your arms and legs to place the ball between your knees.

head and shoulders resting

legs at 90–90

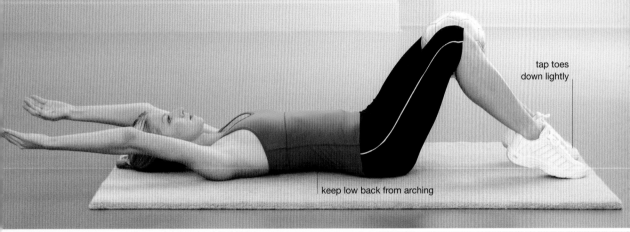

15b Inhale, lowering your arms and feet towards the floor without arching your back. Tap toes down, then exhale as you lift your limbs again to grasp the ball in your hands and return to start. This is 1 rep. Repeat Steps 15a and 15b for a total of 5 reps, then stretch out long, holding the ball behind your head (see end of Step 11).

tap toes
down lightly

keep low back from arching

16 **Balancing side crunch** In neutral position, place the ball under one foot and extend the other leg (inset). With the hands behind the head and the elbows wide, exhale and lift the shoulder blade, twisting that shoulder towards the knee as the working leg bends to meet the elbow. Do this 10 times. Change sides and repeat.

push through heel to
stabilize leg on ball

keep upper arm anchored on floor

17 **Sphinx** Turn onto your stomach and draw your shoulder blades down and together. Lift your chest, position your elbows directly under your shoulders and hold the ball between your hands. Reach the top of your head to the ceiling while you breathe into the stretch, lengthening through the torso.

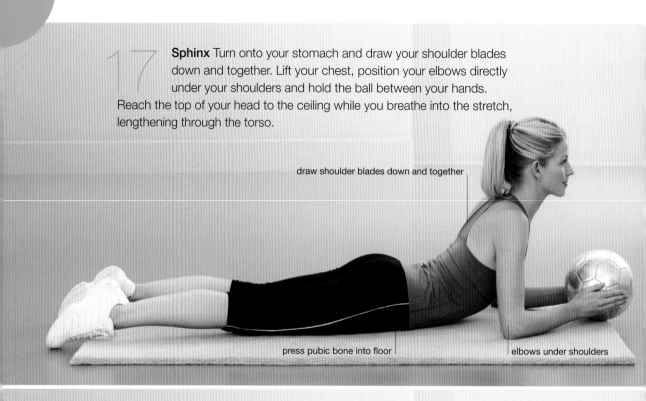

draw shoulder blades down and together

press pubic bone into floor

elbows under shoulders

18 **Forearm plank** From the Sphinx, with your shoulders anchored and still holding the ball, scoop out your abs and lift your hips, making a straight line from shoulder to knee. Keep your shoulder blades wide and apart, head and neck aligned with your spine. To increase the intensity, tuck your toes under and lift your knees.

lift hips

draw abs tight

relax your hands on the ball

Child's pose Bend your knees and reach back with your hips, curving your spine until your buttocks rest on your heels. At the same time, straighten your arms to the front, reaching the ball forwards and lower your forehead towards the floor (inset). Then roll the ball to one side and, still reaching with it, hold the stretch. Repeat to the other side.

keep reaching for the ball

Back extension Holding the ball with both hands, slide forwards onto your stomach, legs hip-width apart. Move the ball to your low back, holding it with fingers pointing back, elbows bent to the ceiling (inset). Rest your forehead on the mat. Inhale, then exhale, lift your chest and straighten your arms, pressing the ball down your back. Inhale, then bend your arms to return. Repeat 10 times.

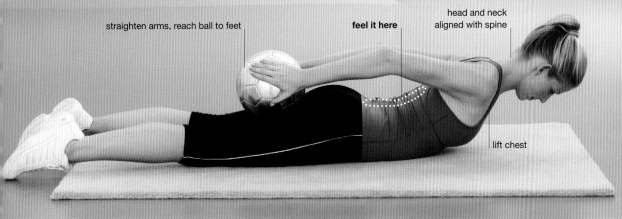

straighten arms, reach ball to feet

feel it here

head and neck aligned with spine

lift chest

>> **floor** bridge stretch/low-back stretch

21 **Bridge stretch** Turn onto your back, knees bent, feet on the floor. Lift your hips and place the ball under the sacrum, allowing it to support your body weight. Inhale and on the exhale feel the low back relax. Hold the ball with your hands if necessary. Take several deep breaths.

body weight rests on ball

22 **Low-back stretch** From the Bridge stretch, bring one knee up over your chest and then the other. Separate the knees, still allowing the ball to support you. Continue to hold onto the ball or turn your palms up and rest your arms by your sides. With every exhale, let your body weight sink into the ball. To come out of the stretch, hold onto the ball and lower one leg at a time.

relax the low back

sit up straight

use hand on opposite knee

23 **Seated spinal twist** Sitting with your legs crossed and hips firmly on the ground, place the ball behind you. Reach one arm back, place your hand on the ball and use your front hand on the opposite knee to deepen the twist. Hold the position and breathe into it, then change sides.

keep hips firmly planted

24 **Forward bend** Return to centre and bring the ball to the front. With your sitbones anchored on the floor, bend forwards, rounding your spine, and reaching the ball to the front with your arms straight. Breathe into the stretch (inset). Then roll the ball to one side, torso facing your knee and hold. Repeat to the other side and return to centre.

ball extends reach

sitbones down evenly

▲ **Floor**
Roll-back
& lift,
page 47

▲ **Warm-up** Hamstring curl,
page 46

▲ **Warm-up** Body sway,
page 46

▲ **Floor** Roll-back & lift, page 47

▲ **Floor** Sphinx,
page 54

ng side crunch, page 53

▲ **Floor** Forearm plank, page 54

beach ball at a glance

▲ **Warm-up** March in place, page 44

▲ **Warm-up** Step-touch in, page 44

▲ **Warm-up** Toe-tap out, page 45

▲ **Warm-up** Twisting knee lift, page 45

▲ **Floor** Toe tap, page 52

▲ **Floor** Ball transfer, pages 52 and 53

▲ **Floor** Ball transfer, pages 52 and 53

▲ **Floor** Balanc

beach ball >>

15 minute **summary**

▲ **Floor** Reverse crunch combo, pages 50 and 51

▲ **Floor** Reverse crunch combo, pages 50 and 51

▲ **Floor** Reverse crunch combo, pages 50 and 51

▲ **Floor** Trunk twist, page 51

▲ **Floor** Seated spinal twist, page 57

ack stretch, page 56

▲ **Floor** Forward bend, page 57

▲ **Floor**
Side twist,
page 48

▲ **Floor** Spinal twist, page 48

▲ **Floor**
Pullover
crunch,
page 49

▲ **Floor** Side reach, page 49

▲ **Floor** Child's
pose, page 55

▲ **Floor** Back extension, page 55

▲ **Floor** Bridge
stretch, page 56

▲ **Floor** Low-b

>> **beach ball** FAQs

As you become familiar with your abs routines, you'll naturally want to know how often and how hard you need to work to get the best results. You may wonder what you should expect to feel after a workout, when you can expect to see change and when you should change the routine.

>> Can I do abs routines every day?

The abs recover quickly from an abundance of training, but still need time to rest and rebuild. Like any muscle group, they require 24 to 48 hours' recovery time between workouts, so you should train them on nonconsecutive days, three to four days per week. For a little extra strengthening stimulus every day, engage your abs as you go about your daily routines (see pp122–123).

>> If I do these exercises faithfully, when will I begin to notice change?

Doing these routines three to four times a week for four to eight weeks will strengthen and firm the muscles. For the sculpting effect to show, you also need to reduce your body fat to reveal the contours of the muscles underneath. You can shed the fat by regularly expending more calories than you consume – incorporate at least 30 minutes of moderate cardio activity most (at least five) days of the week and monitor your dietary intake.

>> How do I know when to change the routine?

You should change the routine every four to eight weeks to continue to stimulate the muscles. If you've been sticking to just one of the routines, pick another one. If you've already been doing several, try changing the order in which you do them, to surprise the muscles. Or use different combinations of the routines on different days of the week.

I've been doing crunches for a while and no longer feel my abs working. They're not nearly as toned as I would like and I can't seem to fatigue them.

If you're not feeling resistance when you perform crunches, you may be making mistakes in technique. You could be crunching too quickly or lifting from your neck and shoulders rather than from your torso. Be sure to contract your abs and connect the ribs to the hips before you lift your torso. Maintain the contraction as you lift and lower, keeping tension in the muscle during the entire set of repetitions.

The day after I do an abs class I'm really in pain. Should my abs be so sore?

You are overdoing it if you are in pain the next day. You want to feel 'muscle awareness', a slight feeling of muscle tenderness that means you targeted the muscles at the proper intensity. To reduce any delayed-onset muscle soreness begin slowly – one routine every other day – and increase gradually.

Will crunches get rid of my ab flab?

You can spot-strengthen and shape a body area, but fat belongs to the whole body and needs to be reduced systemically, through expending more calories (cardio exercise and resistance training) than you consume. And that means following a healthy diet as well.

Am I burning calories when I do crunches?

Yes, you burn calories whenever you exert yourself physically. However, the more lasting advantage of doing resistance exercises (like crunches) is that by strengthening the muscles you increase your lean-body mass. A lean body burns more calories at rest, so you are effectively raising your resting metabolic rate and burning more calories over the course of the day.

15 minute

Get in touch with your deep abdominals to flatten your belly

core basics
routine >>

>> **warm-up** march in place/step-touch in

1 **March in place** With feet parallel, knees soft, arms by your sides, begin marching. Add the arms, lifting them up, then back down. Turn your palms up on the lift, down on the release. March for 16 reps (1 rep = both sides).

2 **Step-touch in** Step one leg to the side, arms by your sides. Step the other leg in, touching your feet together, bending your elbows to that side and swinging your hands to shoulder height. Repeat, moving from side to side, for 8 reps.

turn palms down as you lower arms

keep knee low

bend elbows, fists to shoulder height

shift weight from side to side

3 **Toe-tap out** Step your feet apart, arms by your sides. Swing both arms to one side at shoulder height, coming up on the toes of the opposite foot. Circle your arms down to the other side and reach out with the tapping leg. Repeat, alternating sides for 8 reps.

4 **Twisting knee lift** With legs apart, raise the arms sideways to shoulder height. Bend elbows to 90°, palms forwards. Keeping the back straight, bend one knee to hip height. Rotate your torso, bringing the opposite elbow towards the raised knee. Repeat, alternating sides for 8 reps.

arms swing like a pendulum

reach tapping leg to the side

hold torso upright

lift knee to hip height

>> **warm-up** hamstring curl/body sway

5 **Hamstring curl**
Take your legs wider and reach your arms sideways at shoulder level, palms down. Bend one knee behind and reach for your foot with the opposite hand, raising the other arm up on a diagonal. Repeat, alternating sides for 8 reps.

stretch the fingers

reach hand to foot

6 **Body sway** With legs apart and arms raised, step one leg in, flexing at the waist and head centred between your arms. Repeat, alternating sides for 8 reps.

keep shoulder blades down

torso and head move as one

Repeat Steps 5–1 (reverse order) to complete your warm-up.

expand belly

Pelvic tilt Lie in neutral position, knees bent at 90°, hip-width apart and feet flat on the floor. Rest your arms by your sides, palms up. Begin with a belly breath (inset), then exhale forcefully, compress your abdomen and rotate your pelvis backwards, pressing your low back to the floor. Hold for a moment, then release. Repeat for 10 reps.

compress abs

press low back to floor

Straight-leg lowering In neutral position, do a strong Pelvic tilt and release halfway so your low back goes into its natural curve. Keep your abs tight to stabilize your pelvis in this position. Extend one leg to the height of the other knee (inset). Inhale and slowly lower the leg towards the floor; exhale and return to start. Repeat 6 times, then change sides.

feel it here

draw shoulder blades
down and together

lower leg without resting

>> **floor** 90–90/alternating kicks

9 **90–90** Begin in neutral. Reposition the Pelvic tilt and release halfway, keeping your abs engaged. With your pelvis stabilized, bring one knee up over your hip (inset) and then the other, keeping your calves parallel to the floor. Hold this 90° angle at both the hip and the knee. You should feel strain in your lower abs.

knees over hips

calves parallel to the floor

10 **Alternating kicks** From 90–90, bring one knee in over your chest and straighten the other leg, lowering it as close to the floor as possible without arching your back. Pause, then return to the start position and repeat, alternating legs for 5 reps. Hug your knees into your chest and rock from side to side.

bring knee over chest

lengthen leg towards the floor

11 **Knee drop** Come into 90–90, abs strong, pelvis stable, arms resting by your sides and palms up. Press your knees and feet together (inset). Inhale as you rotate your pelvis to one side, lowering your knees halfway to the floor. Exhale and return to centre. Continue, alternating sides, for 6 reps.

tighten abs as you rotate pelvis

legs together, knees and ankles stacked

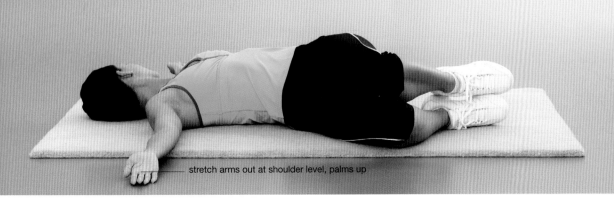

12 **Spinal twist** Bring your feet to the floor in neutral position, then rotate your knees to one side. Stretch your arms out to the sides at shoulder level, palms up. Rest, turning your head to the opposite side. Hold the position briefly and breathe, then change sides.

stretch arms out at shoulder level, palms up

>> **floor** double-leg lowering

bend legs at 90–90

extend legs to ceiling

13a Double-leg lowering

Return to 90–90, arms by your sides and palms up to keep your shoulders open (inset). Extend both legs to the ceiling and point your toes. Draw your abs tight to stabilize the top of your pelvis against the floor, low back in neutral position.

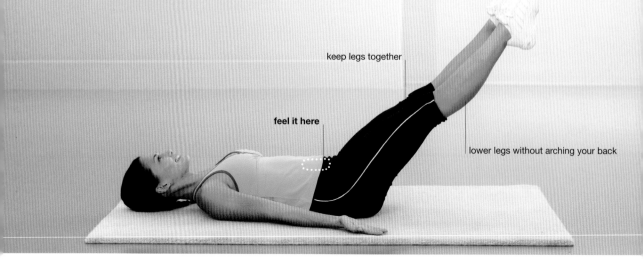

13b

Exhale as you lower both legs towards the floor, going as far as you can without arching your low back. Keep pulling your abs in as you go. Inhale, bend your knees in and return to start. Repeat 10 times. Hug your knees in to rest.

keep legs together

feel it here

lower legs without arching your back

press arm back

14 **Spiral ab twist** Sit on one hip, legs bent to the other side, front foot aligned with the opposite knee. Plant your supporting hand on the ground in line with your shoulder and extend your other arm up on a diagonal. Look up at your hand. Inhale and press your raised arm back to stretch your torso (inset). Exhale, contract your abs and curl the raised arm under the supporting arm. Repeat 8 times, then change sides and repeat 8 times.

feel it here

curl shoulder in, reach arm through

feel it here

15 **Roll-back** Sit up straight, knees bent at 90°, feet flat. Pull your torso in close to your thighs. Reach your arms forwards at shoulder level, palms down (inset). Exhale and take your belly button to your spine as you roll back onto your tailbone. Inhale and realign your spine to straighten up. If you need help, use your hands on your thighs. Repeat for 4 reps.

feel it here

curve the spine, ribs to hips

16 **Twisting roll-back** Add a twist! With your arms extended (inset), perform a roll-back, curving your spine into a 'C'. Then twist your torso to one side, bending your elbow and pulling it back. Reach both arms forwards to return to start. Repeat on the other side, alternating sides for 4 reps.

bend elbow back at
shoulder level

17 **Lengthening stretch** Holding onto your thighs, roll down to the floor and extend your arms and legs. Take a deep breath in and stretch out as far as you can. Exhale and relax. Cross one ankle over the other and take the wrist on the same side in your other hand. Pull to the opposite side, creating a stretch down one side of your body. Repeat on the other side.

take wrist in hand and
pull to the side

18 **Kneeling lift** Kneel on all fours, wrists under shoulders, knees under hips. Extend one leg to hip height, then lift the opposite arm to shoulder level. Stabilize the supporting arm by spreading your fingers and pushing into your thumb and index finger (inset). Hold, then lower and lift your limbs 6 times and hold again. Repeat on the other side.

touch down lightly without resting

19 **Forearm plank** From the kneeling position, take your hands forwards and place your forearms on the floor, elbows directly under your shoulders. Take your knees back and drop your hips, creating a straight line from shoulder to knee. Pull your abs tight and anchor your shoulder blades (inset). Hold, then straighten your legs and come onto your toes in the full forearm plank position. Hold.

anchor shoulder blades

tuck toes under

elbows under shoulders

touch both knees down

20 **Forearm plank plus** From the full plank, lower both knees simultaneously 4 times (inset). Then lower one knee at a time, alternating sides for 4 reps. If you are fatiguing, just try to hold the forearm plank from the knees. Breathe naturally throughout.

keep hips level

touch down one knee at a time

21 **Child's pose** Sit back into child's pose, with your hips to your heels and your forehead to the floor. Stretch your arms forwards. Take a few seconds to rest in this position and refresh yourself. Breathe deeply, releasing tension from your muscles with every exhale.

hips to heels

forehead towards floor

22 **Side plank** Lie on your side, resting on your forearm, elbow beneath shoulder, legs bent behind you, top hand on your hip (inset). Contract your abs, exhale and lift your hips. Hold, then lower and lift for a total of 4 times. Lower to the floor without resting.

knees stacked, legs bent behind

feel it here

elbow under shoulder

23 **Side plank with clam** Now add a 'clam' to challenge your balance and stability. Open and close your top knee 4 times. Be sure to keep your rib cage lifted and the shoulder of your supporting arm down. Breathe naturally.

keep hips stable

24 **Side stretch** Lower your hips to the floor and sit up. Separating your legs, bend your knees to the side and reach your opposite arm overhead, palm down. Stretch out the muscles that you just worked, especially the obliques and then repeat Steps 22–24 on the other side.

keep shoulder blade down

weight on front hip

25 **Wide 'V' stretch** Sit tall and open your legs in a wide 'V' (inset). Lean forwards from your hips with your spine straight and reach your arms to centre. Keeping both hips planted evenly on the floor, lift your spine, then turn your torso to face one leg and hold. Pass through centre and repeat on the other side.

spine straight

hips firmly planted

core basics >>

core basics at a glance

▲ **Warm-up** March in place, page 68

▲ **Warm-up** Step-touch in, page 68

▲ **Warm-up** Toe-tap out, page 69

▲ **Warm-up** Twisting knee lift, page 69

▲ **Floor** Twisting roll-back, page 76

▲ **Floor** Lengthening stretch, page 76

▲ **Floor** Kneeling lift, page 77

▲ **Floor** Forear

▲ **Floor**
Pelvic tilt,
page 71

▲ **Warm-up** Hamstring curl,
page 70

▲ **Warm-up** Body sway,
page 70

▲ **Floor**
Straight-leg lowering, page 71

▲ **Floor** Forearm plank
plus, page 78

n plank, page 77

▲ **Floor** Child's pose, page 78

26 **Seated spinal twist** Bring your legs together, extended in front of you, torso facing forwards. Bend one leg in, knee to ceiling and cross it over the other, extended leg. Reach the arm on the same side as the bent knee behind you, hand on the floor (inset), then twist your torso towards it, using the other arm on your knee to deepen the stretch. Hold, then switch sides.

use opposite arm on bent knee

27 **Forward bend** Turn your torso back to centre. Straighten your spine, lift up and out of the low back and then reach your head forwards. Relax over your knees, breathing deeply.

round over legs

knees straight but not locked

15 minute **summary**

▲ **Floor**
Double-leg
lowering,
page 74

▲ **Floor** Double-leg lowering, page 74

▲ **Floor** Spiral
ab twist,
page 75

▲ **Floor** Roll-back, page 75

▲ **Floor** Seated spinal
twist, page 81

'V' stretch, page 80

▲ **Floor** Forward bend, page 81

▲ **Floor**
90–90,
page 72

▲ **Floor**
Knee drop,
page 73

▲ **Floor** Alternating kicks, page 72

▲ **Floor** Spinal twist, page 73

▲ **Floor** Side
plank, page 79

▲ **Floor** Side plank with clam, page 79

▲ **Floor** Side
stretch, page 80

▲ **Floor** Wide

>> **core basics** FAQs

Core training has been making headlines recently, but what exactly is it and how does it differ from more traditional abdominal exercises? This section addresses questions related to your core, why it is important to strengthen it and the types of exercises that are most effective at targeting it.

>> What exactly is core training?

Technically, core training focuses on developing and balancing the muscles in the anatomical centre of the body – the core. Core training is an integrated approach to working the muscles of the torso and pelvis and training them to function as a unit, instead of in isolation.

>> Why is core training so important? How will I benefit differently from doing more traditional types of abdominal exercises, like crunches?

Core training engages the abs and spinal extensors to function as a team to provide support for the spine and maintain its proper alignment. Core exercises train the spine for stability in all positions against gravity – as in the Kneeling lift (p77) and Side plank with clam (p79). Crunches, on the other hand, are a weight-supported exercise that isolates one abdominal muscle, the rectus abdominis. It is less involved and, therefore, less physically demanding.

>> Is anything wrong with the way we did exercises before core training emerged?

No. There are benefits to doing classic exercises that isolate a muscle as well as doing core exercises. The Side crunch (p25), for instance, works the obliques in isolation, whereas the Side twist using the ball (p48) recruits the muscles of the abdomen and the back to stabilize the spine while the obliques perform the twist. Doing different exercises will keep your routine fresh.

>> **I've seen a lot of core-training routines in magazines that are based on yoga and Pilates. Are these the only ways to train the core?**

Both these disciplines focus on using core strength, but the concepts are not limited to them. The routines in this book offer a unique blend of exercises to target the core, including some techniques from yoga and Pilates. Often, exercise techniques evolve and are used in more than one method of exercise. The blend of methods enhances the variety in your workout.

>> **How do I know if I'm working my core? What should I be feeling?**

To get in touch with the deepest abdominals, do a few belly breaths (p16) with your hands on your lower abdomen. Feel the belly expand and contract, then return to neutral. When you are working the core, the belly is neither hollowed in nor pushed out. Your abs should feel taut or stiff to the touch, as if someone punched you in the belly and you reacted by tightening the muscles.

>> **How do I know if I have a weak core?**

Your ability to stabilize your pelvis in neutral position is a good indicator of core strength. First, identify where neutral spine alignment is for your body; then see if you can maintain the proper alignment of the low back against resistance (see pp16–17). If you have a weak core, you will notice that your pelvis will tip from side to side or your low back will arch off the floor.

>> **How does core training affect the muscles in my arms and legs? Will it keep them in shape?**

Any exercise where you are supporting your body weight against gravity will provide resistance training for your arms and legs. These include all the plank and side plank variations, the Kneeling lift (p77) and Kneeling crunch (p99).

15 minute

Challenge your core
with this more
advanced routine
when you are ready

core challenge
routine >>

>> **warm-up** march in place/step-touch in

1 **March in place** With feet parallel, knees soft and arms by your sides, begin marching. Add the arms, lifting them up, with palms up, then down, with palms down. March for 16 reps (1 rep = both sides).

2 **Step-touch in** Step one leg to the side, arms by your sides. Step the other leg in, touching your feet together, bending your elbows to that side and swinging your hands to shoulder height. Repeat, moving from side to side, for 8 reps.

turn palms down as you lower arms

keep knee low

bend elbows, fists to shoulder height

shift weight from side to side

Toe-tap out Step your feet apart, arms by your sides. Swing both arms to one side at shoulder height, coming up on the toes of the opposite foot. Circle your arms down to the other side and reach out with the tapping leg. Repeat, alternating sides for 8 reps.

Twisting knee lift With legs apart, raise the arms sideways to shoulder height. Bend your elbows to 90°, palms forwards. With a straight back, bend one knee to hip height. Rotate your torso, bringing the opposite elbow towards the raised knee. Repeat, alternating sides for 8 reps.

arms swing like a pendulum

reach tapping leg to the side

hold torso upright

lift knee to hip height

>> **warm-up** hamstring curl/body sway

5 Hamstring curl

Take your legs wider and reach your arms out to the sides at shoulder level, palms down. Bend one knee behind and reach for your foot with the opposite hand, raising the other arm up on a diagonal. Repeat, alternating sides for 8 reps.

stretch the fingers

reach hand to foot

6 Body sway

With legs apart and arms raised, step one leg in and flex at the waist. Keep your head centred between your arms. Repeat, alternating sides for 8 reps.

keep shoulder blades down

torso and head move as one

Repeat Steps 5–1 (reverse order) to complete your warm-up.

>> **floor** double crunch

7a **Double crunch** Raise one leg at a time to 90–90, knees above hips, calves parallel to the floor and with a right angle at hips and knees (see p17). Place your hands unclasped behind your head. Exhale and lift the shoulder blades, keeping the abs tight.

legs at 90–90

shoulder blades clear the floor

7b Hold the position as you curl your hips. Release the hips and then the shoulders, without resting your head on the floor. Repeat 10 times, then hug your knees in to stretch your back.

right angle at knees

curl hips off floor

shoulders stay lifted

>> **floor** tuck & roll/bridge

heels to floor

8 **Tuck & roll** Lying in 90–90, legs together, arms by your sides, palms up, exhale, draw your abs in, then lower your legs and touch your heels lightly to the mat (inset). Inhale, return to start, then exhale and roll your hips to the side, lowering your knees halfway. Inhale and return. Repeat the abs tuck, heels to the floor, then roll to other side. Continue alternating sides for a total of 3 reps (1 rep = tuck/roll/tuck/roll).

legs together

shoulders stay open

rotate halfway to floor

spine in neutral

9 **Bridge** Begin in neutral position, knees bent at 90°, hip-width apart, feet flat and arms by your sides, palms up (inset). Inhale, then exhale, press your low back to the floor and begin lifting your hips, peeling your back off the floor until your hips form a straight line with your knees and shoulders. Inhale and release down one vertebra at a time. Repeat 3 times.

maintain neutral spine

90–90 position

10 **Crunch & extend** Begin in 90–90, hands behind your head (inset). Exhale, lift your chest to bring your shoulder blades off the floor at the same time as you extend your legs to 45°, without arching your low back. Inhale, and release back to start, keeping tension in your abs throughout. Repeat 5 times. Hug your knees to rest.

elbows wide

feel it here

legs at 45° angle to floor

11 **Dead bug** Again, begin in 90–90, arms extended towards the ceiling, palms forwards. Pull your abs tight, belly button to spine (inset). Exhale, lower your opposite arm and leg towards the floor, bringing the other knee in over your chest. Switch sides for 6 reps, then add a hold for another 4 reps. Breathe naturally throughout. Hug your knees briefly.

bring knee over chest

feel it here

lower without resting

lower without resting

core challenge >>

12 **Spinal arch & curve** Kneel on all fours, wrists under shoulders, knees under hips, spine in neutral alignment. Exhale and round your back up to the ceiling, dropping your head between your arms and tucking your hips under (inset). Inhale, lifting your head and hips and curving your spine into a 'C'. Repeat twice each way.

wrists under shoulders

knees under hips

13 **Kneeling twist** On all fours, stabilize one arm, spreading the fingers and pushing into the thumb and index finger to create a base of support. Place your other hand behind your head (inset). Exhale and rotate your torso, elbow and head twisting as one. Inhale and return to start. Repeat 6 times.

stabilize your arm

keep hips still

feel it here

press into thumb and index finger

stabilize supporting arm

rotate arm, palm up

14 **Kneeling crunch** Kneeling, one arm stabilized as in Step 13, extend the other arm forwards at shoulder level and the opposite leg back at hip height (inset). Exhale, contract your abs and round your back up to the ceiling as you draw elbow to knee, turning the palm up. Repeat 6 times, then switch sides and repeat Steps 13 and 14.

15 **Plank with leg lift** From a kneeling position, bend your elbows under your shoulders, hands in loose fists. Straighten one leg behind you, then the other. Contract the abs. Your body should form a straight line from shoulders to heels (inset). Exhale and lift one leg, keeping the knee straight, then place that leg back down and lift the other. Continue for 6 reps, then sit back in Child's pose (Step 25).

hands in loose fists

keep hips level

look up at hand

16 **Twisting side plank** Lie on your side, hips stacked, bottom knee bent behind, top leg straight and foot flexed. Plant your elbow under your shoulder, forearm on floor, hand in loose fist. Tighten your abs and lift your hips. Extend your top arm to the ceiling and look up at it (inset). Exhale and twist, reaching your arm under your torso. Return to start and repeat for a total of 6 times.

feel it here

head follows action

feel it here

17 **Overhead reach** Still in the side plank, reach your top arm overhead, palm down, stretching out the obliques while your core muscles work to maintain this position. Keep your head and neck aligned with your spine. Hold the stretch briefly.

hips stacked

abs tight

rib cage lifted

keep shoulder blade down

weight on front hip

18 Seated side stretch
Lower your hips from the side plank and come into a seated position with one leg bent behind and the other bent in front. Reach the arm on the same side as the front leg overhead towards the back knee, palm down. Hold for a moment, then swing your legs around to the other side to repeat Steps 16–18.

19 **Toe dip** Sit tall, both knees bent in front, feet flat. Lean back onto your elbows, shoulder blades down and together. Tighten your abs and slide your hands under your low back for support, palms down. Lift your legs to 90–90 (inset). Inhale and dip your toes to the mat, maintaining the right angle at the knees. Exhale and return to start. Repeat 5 times.

anchor shoulder blades

tap toes lightly

shoulder blade down

lift up through rib cage

crunch ribs to hips

20 **Balance & crunch**
Balance on your hip and elbow, top hand behind your head, and bring your feet off the floor (inset). Exhale and contract the obliques, drawing the top elbow to the knees. Repeat 10 times, then repeat on the other side.

21 **Crossover stretch** Stretch out on your back. Bend one knee up and use the opposite hand to guide it across your body into a Spinal twist. Turn your head away from the bent knee. Rest the other arm to the side, palm up. Relax into the stretch, then change sides.

use hand to deepen stretch

22 **Low-back stretch** Still lying on your back, return to centre. Bend both knees up over your chest, separate them and place your hands under your thighs. Inhale, then exhale as you pull your knees towards your shoulders, lifting your tailbone off the floor to gently stretch out your low back.

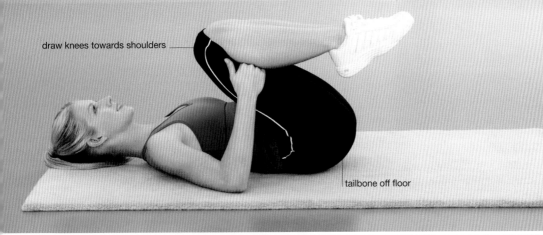

draw knees towards shoulders

tailbone off floor

23 **Circles** Place your hands on top of your knees (inset) and circle them together 3 times each way, massaging your low back into the floor. Breathe naturally throughout and, with every exhale, think of releasing tension in your muscles.

circle knees together

24 **Lat push** Turn onto your stomach, arms bent wide to the sides. Tuck your toes under, push onto the balls of your feet, knees off the floor. Scoop out your abs, draw your shoulders together in a 'W' and lift your arms and head (inset). Push one arm forwards, then bring it back, alternating sides for a total of 5 reps.

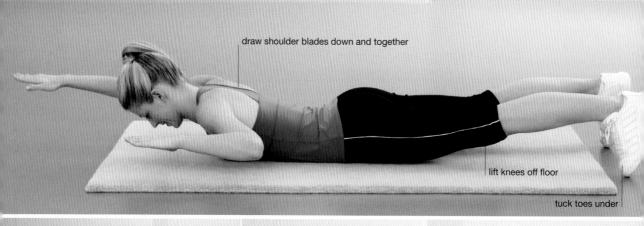

draw shoulder blades down and together

lift knees off floor

tuck toes under

25 **Child's pose** Sit back on your heels and bend forwards, arms stretching centre. Keep your elbows off the mat to get the best stretch. Take deep breaths and relax into the position (inset). Then, keeping your head centred between your elbows, walk your hands to one side and hold. Repeat to the other side.

keep hips down

head between elbows

elbows off floor

26 **Alligator** Come to a kneeling position, wrists under shoulders, knees under hips, spine in neutral alignment. Inhale, turn your head towards your hip. Exhale and return to centre. Inhale to the other side; exhale and return. Continue moving from side to side, using the breath to guide you, for a total of 3 reps.

shoulders and hips move

27 **Thread the needle** This is a Spinal twist from the knees. Starting on all fours, 'thread' one arm under your body to the opposite side, palm up. Come to rest on your shoulder and the side of your head. Breathe into the stretch, feeling the elongation all along your side. Then change sides and thread the needle the other way.

rest on shoulder and side of head

▲ **Floor**
Double
crunch,
page 95

▲ **Warm-up** Hamstring curl,
page 94

▲ **Warm-up** Body sway,
page 94

▲ **Floor** Double crunch, page 95

▲ **Floor** Balance &
crunch, page 102

, page 101

▲ **Floor** Crossover stretch, page 102

core challenge at a glance

▲ **Warm-up** March in place, page 92

▲ **Warm-up** Step-touch in, page 92

▲ **Warm-up** Toe-tap out, page 93

▲ **Warm-up** Twisting knee lift, page 93

▲ **Floor** Twisting side plank, page 100

▲ **Floor** Overhead reach, page 100

▲ **Floor** Seated side stretch, page 101

▲ **Floor** Toe dip

core challenge >>

15 minute **summary**

▲ **Floor**
Spinal arch
& curve,
page 98

▲ **Floor** Kneeling twist, page 98

▲ **Floor**
Kneeling
crunch,
page 99

▲ **Floor** Plank with leg lift, page 99

▲ **Floor** Alligator,
page 105

pose, page 104

▲ **Floor** Thread the needle, page 105

▲ **Floor**
Tuck & roll,
page 96

▲ **Floor** Bridge, page 96

▲ **Floor**
Crunch &
extend,
page 97

▲ **Floor** Dead bug, page 97

▲ **Floor** Low-back
stretch, page 103

▲ **Floor** Circles, page 103

▲ **Floor** Lat push,
page 104

▲ **Floor** Child's

>> **core challenge** FAQs

This section deals with reducing the size of the belly. Why is it that an apple shape is at greater risk for disease than the pear? Why is abdominal fat considered 'toxic' and what can we do about it? Does belly fat contribute to low-back pain? And how do you recover a flat tummy after giving birth?

>> Why is the mid-section of the body the part that goes out of shape so quickly?

There is a natural tendency to store fat in the abdominal area and this can make it difficult to see the results of your hard work. Many other variables influence the size and shape of your abdomen as well, including genetics, gender, age and abdominal surgery (see p10). Remind yourself of all the benefits of strengthening these muscles and stay focused on the positive results you can achieve.

>> What causes the midlife belly?

Age is one part of the equation; hormones and stress also contribute. With age, a woman's level of oestrogen declines and the male hormone, testosterone, becomes more prominent. This causes fat to migrate to the gut from other parts of the body (the hips, for example). Stress reaction has a similar effect on fat distribution as it releases another hormone, cortisol, which also encourages fat storage in the belly.

>> Why is abdominal fat so 'toxic'?

Fat found deep in the abdomen (visceral fat) is the real culprit. The enzymes in abdominal fat cells are very active, allowing fat to move easily into and out of the cells. The greater the amount of fat in the abdominal cavity, the more that can be dumped into the bloodstream, contributing to high cholesterol levels and heart disease. Additionally, a stress response increases the enzyme activity and causes fat to be released into the blood. (To measure your own risk, see pp116–117.)

Can exercise help reduce toxic fat?

Yes! Actually, visceral fat is easier to reduce than fat from your thighs (subcutaneous fat). It responds more rapidly to exercise and diet because it is more active and breaks down more quickly. Research shows that exercise reduces the size of fat cells in the belly more effectively than dieting alone. It also prevents fat from being stored in the organs and muscles.

What's the fastest way to shape up my mid-section?

The optimal programme includes cardio training (at least 30 minutes a day, five days a week), abdominal strengthening and stretching (as in these workouts) and eating a moderate diet. Begin gradually and build up slowly, in both the cardio and the abs routines. To speed results, always aim for slightly higher intensity. When you are ready to progress, do more intense cardio work to burn more calories in the same period of time; and double up on the abs workouts (just remember to allow a day of rest before repeating them).

Will doing these exercises help prevent low-back ache?

They definitely can help. A combination of weak abdominals and extra weight around the belly can pull the top of the pelvis forwards, increasing the curve in the low back and straining it. This can cause muscle fatigue, soreness or injury. Solution – strengthen the abs and lose body fat.

I'm a new mother. What's the best way to get my flat belly back?

It may take up to six weeks for your body to recover from giving birth, and many factors can interfere with regaining your pre-baby body, including age, skin elasticity, C-section scars, former fitness level and multiple births. When your doctor gives you permission, resume activity gradually (abs routines and cardio workouts). Also remember to engage your abs and use proper body mechanics when carrying, changing and lifting the baby (see pp122–123).

15 minute

abs
roundup >>

Keeping your abs in shape
enhances your health, fitness
and quality of life

>> **risk** assessment

Before beginning any exercise programme, make sure that it is safe for you. Take the PAR-Q questionnaire opposite to see if you should check with your doctor first. Then take the measurements here to assess whether the body-fat distribution in your trunk poses a health risk.

Body composition and shape are closely related to fitness and health. Check your body shape in the mirror: if you have excess body fat, are you carrying it around your middle (apple shape) or does it settle in your hips and thighs (pear shape)? Excess deep abdominal fat, carried at the belly, signals a greater risk of heart disease, high blood pressure and diabetes than ample hips. Exercise can help reduce your risk. Be sure to perform regular, calorie-burning cardio along with your abs routines.

Measuring the risk

Take a measurement at your waist. The waist circumference alone can be used as an indicator of health risk because, as we have seen, abdominal obesity is the issue. Measure your waist at the narrowest point on your belly. A measurement above 89cm (35in) is considered high risk for women; above 99cm (39in) is high risk for men.

Another simple method of determining body-fat distribution is the Waist-to-Hip Ratio. Take a measurement at the largest part of your hips (see photo inset); then divide your waist measurement (see right) by your hip measurement to determine the ratio. For example:

Waist measurement = 76cm (30in)
Hip measurement = 102cm (40in)
Waist-to-Hip Ratio = 76 ÷ 102 (30 ÷ 40) = 0.75

Health risk increases with a high Waist-to-Hip Ratio: in women aged 20–39, a ratio of more than 0.79 is considered high; for women aged 40–59, the figure is 0.82; and for those aged 60–69, it is 0.84.

To take accurate measurements, always use a flexible plastic or cloth tape measure and be sure to keep it level as you wrap it round your body.

PAR-Q AND YOU   A questionnaire for people aged 15 to 69   Physical Activity Readiness Questionnaire – PAR-Q (revised 2002)

Regular physical activity is fun and healthy and increasingly more people are starting to become more active every day. Being more active is perfectly safe for most people. However, some people should check with their doctor before they start becoming much more physically active than they are already.

If you are planning to become much more physically active than you are now, start by answering the seven questions in the box below. If you are between the ages of 15 and 69, the PAR-Q will tell you if you should check with your doctor before you start. If you are over 69 years of age and you are not used to being very active, check with your doctor.

Common sense is your best guide when you answer these questions. Please read the questions carefully and answer each one honestly: check YES or NO.

YES   NO

☐ ☐ **1** Has your doctor ever said that you have a heart condition <u>and</u> that you should only do physical activity recommended by a doctor?

☐ ☐ **2** Do you feel pain in your chest when you do physical activity?

☐ ☐ **3** In the past month, have you had chest pain when you were not doing physical activity?

☐ ☐ **4** Do you lose your balance because of dizziness or do you ever lose consciousness?

YES   NO

☐ ☐ **5** Do you have a bone or joint problem (for example, back, knee or hip) that could possibly be made worse by a marked change in your physical activity?

☐ ☐ **6** Is your doctor currently prescribing drugs (for example, water pills) for your blood pressure or heart condition?

☐ ☐ **7** Do you know of any other reason why you should not do physical activity?

If you answered YES to one or more questions

Talk with your doctor by phone or in person BEFORE you start becoming much more physically active or BEFORE you have a fitness appraisal.
Tell your doctor about the PAR-Q and which questions you answered YES.
• You may be able to do any activity you want – as long as you start slowly and build up gradually. Or, you may need to restrict your activities to those which are safe for you. Talk with your doctor about the kinds of activities you wish to participate in and follow his/her advice.
• Find out which community programmes are going to prove safe and helpful for you.

If you answered NO to all questions

If you answered NO honestly to all PAR-Q questions, you can be reasonably sure that you can:
• start becoming much more physically active – begin slowly and build up gradually. This is the safest and easiest way to go.
• take part in a fitness appraisal – this is an excellent way to determine your basic fitness so that you can plan the best way for you to exercise and live actively. It is also highly recommended that you have your blood pressure evaluated. If your reading is over 144/94, talk with your doctor before you start becoming much more physically active.

DELAY BECOMING MUCH MORE ACTIVE:
• if you are not feeling well because of a temporary illness such as a cold or a fever – wait until you feel better.
• if you are or may be pregnant – talk to your doctor before you start becoming more active.

PLEASE NOTE:
If your health changes so that you then answer YES to any of the above questions, tell your fitness or health professional. Ask whether you should change your physical activity plan.

>> **abs work** for fitness

A well-rounded exercise programme has a definite structure and
includes cardiovascular or aerobic exercise, resistance training and
stretching. Your *15-minute Abs Workout* is really a form of resistance
training that develops both strength and endurance in the abs.

Every workout should begin with a warm-up to
prepare the muscles for more strenuous work and
reduce the risk of injury. Rhythmic stepping
patterns and arm movements serve to elevate the
temperature of the core body and muscle tissue,
and bathe the joints in lubricating (synovial) fluid.

Resistance training uses various methods of
muscle overload to stimulate muscle development.
In these abs workouts, the overload is provided by
your own body weight. To add resistance, use a
weighted ball in the Beach Ball routine (pp44–57).

The importance of core strength

Core strength is integral to the proper execution of
any exercise in which you are working with your
own body (as opposed to using a machine). In both
the squat and the push-up, for example, strong
abs maintain the neutral alignment of the spine as
you lift and lower your body weight against gravity.
If you combine squats and push-ups with your abs
workout, you have a mini full-body conditioning
routine that you can do any time, any place.

Squat By working the thighs, buttocks and lower legs, as
well as using the abs and back muscles, the squat is the
closest we can get to a full-body exercise.

Push-up This very efficient exercise requires core strength
to keep the torso in alignment as you work the muscles of
the upper body – the chest, shoulders and triceps.

A strong core also enhances your cardio workouts, providing postural support when you are walking, jogging, stair climbing and so on. And conversely, cardio activities are a key factor in burning calories and reducing body fat, especially the 'toxic' fat around the belly (see Risk Assessment, p116). To lose belly fat and flatten the belly, incorporate 30 minutes of cardio most days of the week and do your abs workout every other day.

Stretching is the third component. It restores length to the muscles after they have been contracting in cardio and resistance exercises. It also improves posture and alignment. Targeted stretches can help realign the pelvis and reduce belly pouch. If the hip flexors are tight, for example, they can pull the top of the pelvis forwards, creating excessive sway in the low back and causing your belly to protrude (even if you have no body fat). Lengthening these muscles releases the pelvis into a neutral position. This not only benefits posture, but also helps activate the deepest abdominals. The two stretches shown here can help.

For the Quadriceps stretch (above), lie on your side, bend one knee behind you and draw your foot towards your buttocks. Tuck your hips under to feel the stretch in the hip flexor. For the Kneeling lunge stretch (right), come up on one knee. Press your hips forwards until you feel a stretch in the front of your hip.

>> **perfect** positioning

Positioning refers to how you align your body before moving and how you stabilize it while you perform the exercise. Perfect positioning serves to establish a supportive foundation for the movement, isolate the target muscles for better results and protect the body from injury.

Although the entire body needs to be properly stabilized, we should pay special attention to the spine, neck, shoulder girdle (shoulder blades) and pelvis. To understand your own positioning better, you should first be aware of how you hold these areas when you are at rest. Each body is as individual as its owner, with a unique physical landscape of varying curvatures, limb lengths and joint structure. Learning to know your body at rest will help define the areas you can improve with

training. Be careful not to force your body into an unnatural position that causes pain or discomfort.

Correct alignment

Alignment pertains to the ability to hold your form in all positions against gravity – standing, sitting, on all fours, supine (face-up) and prone (face-down). The head and neck are always held in alignment with the spine. The neck is the most mobile part of your spine and depends on its muscles to support the

Positioning for Forearm plank Stabilize your shoulder blades. Hold your hands in loose fists to relax the upper body. Allow the strength to emanate from your centre.

Positioning for 'W's' Lie face-down, arms bent wide and to the sides. Lift your head slightly. Inhale, then draw the shoulder blades down and together as you slowly exhale.

4.5–5.4kg (10–12lb) weight of the head. A good tip for maintaining alignment when you are in the prone position, as shown in the photographs here, is to remember 'nose down'.

The correct position of the spine is in neutral alignment, with the natural curves in place – an anterior (inward) curve in the neck, a gentle posterior (outward) curve in the upper back, and a slight inward curve again in the low back. The photograph below depicts a lovely neutral spine in the kneeling position. The same alignment applies to standing and floor work as well.

The alignment of the pelvis affects the curve of the low back. In neutral, the pelvis is not tilted forwards or backwards. Tight muscles in the front of the thigh (the quadriceps and hip flexors) can pull the pelvis into an anterior tilt, causing the lower belly to protrude and increasing the curve in the low back (known as 'swayback'). If the hamstrings in the back of the thigh are tight, they can cause a posterior tilt that flattens the curve in the low back. Doing the Pelvic tilt (pp16–17) can help you explore exactly where neutral is for you.

The shoulder girdle is a tricky area, requiring special effort to stabilize properly, given its high degree of mobility. This lack of inherent stability is one reason why our shoulders tend to creep up around our ears and pull forwards in a hunched posture. We need to create stability by strengthening the muscles that retract (pull back) and depress (pull down) the shoulder blades. A number of terms describe this action – bracing, anchoring, pinching. 'W's' are a simple exercise to strengthen these muscles. They are depicted in the prone position on p120, but you can also do them standing or seated. Do 10 of them anytime during the course of your day – at your desk, watching TV – to help reverse the 'forward slouch'. Hold each contraction for a count of five as you exhale.

Perfect positioning when kneeling means keeping your knees under your hips; your wrists under your shoulders; your shoulder blades anchored; your spine in neutral; your abs engaged. When preparing to lift one arm, as for the Kneeling lift (p77), stabilize the supporting arm by pushing into the thumb and index finger of that hand.

>> **abs in everyday** life

Your anatomic centre, or core, generates strength and mobility for the whole body. Muscles maintain the alignment of the skeletal frame when you are sitting, standing and moving. They provide endurance for holding a position and dynamic power when the body is in motion.

The abdominals are key players in core training. The muscles of the spine – the spinal extensors – work in concert with them to stabilize the torso. By strengthening and stretching these opposing muscle groups, you not only improve your figure, but you also improve your ability to function and you reduce your risk of developing musculo-skeletal problems. A strong core equips you to handle the routine physical demands of daily life – lifting children, working at a desk, doing housework, driving a car, or simply getting up out of a chair – with greater ease and comfort.

The abs and spinal extensors also provide postural support for correct alignment of the skeleton. Alignment refers to the relationship of the head, shoulders, spine and hips to each other. Normal alignment counteracts the constant force of gravity on the body, reducing stress on the spine and ensuring that the joints work efficiently. Without proper postural support, your muscles work at a disadvantage in their attempt to support you against gravity, and so you tire more easily. Under strain, they are also at higher risk of injury. Strong abs support the low back and help prevent debilitating pain.

The abs engage the moment you get out of bed and continue working all day. As you develop a kinesthetic awareness of the way they work in your body, it becomes easier consciously to recruit them throughout the day. Using proper body mechanics reduces muscle fatigue and is energizing. You may not feel so tired during the course of your day.

>> **a glossary** of terms

- **Musculo-skeletal system** The bones (skeleton), joints and muscles. All human movement depends on the interaction of these three components.

- **Alignment** The skeletal frame in balance, following the natural curves of the spine, with the segments of the body stacked vertically from head to toe.

- **Body mechanics** Muscles maintain proper alignment of the skeleton in movement to create efficiency of joint action and reduce the risk of strain.

Body mechanics and alignment tips

When sitting, use active, internal abdominal stabilization rather than passive, external support. The torso will passively conform to whatever improper position is available, so you cannot rely on external support. Properly designed chairs and desks are rare. Keep your weight distributed evenly across both hips. Feel the sitbones, not the tailbone, beneath you. Sit up tall, with the spine straight and with a natural curve in the low back. To reverse the forward slouch, activate the shoulder blades, 'pinching' them down and together (see 'W's', p120).

In activities that require pushing and pulling (left), engage your abs to keep your back straight and bend forwards from the hips. Shift your weight in a rocking motion.

When you are standing leaning forwards (below), use your abs to stabilize the torso. For folding laundry, for instance, flex from the hips, keeping the upper back straight.

When standing, distribute your weight evenly on both feet. Soften the knees. Line the ribs up over the hips. Think of pulling up through the abdomen and lengthening through the spine to counteract the force of gravity. Engage the abs to position the pelvis in neutral spine alignment (see pp120–121).

As you walk, balance the head above the shoulders and hips. Keep your rib cage lifted as if there were a string from the centre of your sternum to a second storey. Relax your shoulders down and slightly back.

In activities where you are standing leaning forwards, as in washing up, making the bed, folding laundry, or brushing your teeth, the common tendency is to bend forwards from the waist and round the upper spine, which creates a slumped posture and places a lot of stress on the vertebrae. Instead, retrain yourself to bend the knees slightly and flex forwards from the hip, using your abs to keep the torso straight.

When lifting something heavy, such as a baby from his/her cot or a box from the floor, keep your upper back straight and your low back in neutral position. Tighten the muscles of your abdomen to support the low back and bend your knees. Let the strong muscles of the glutes and legs do the work. Keep the load as close to your body as possible.

In pushing/pulling movements, as when vacuuming, mopping the floor or raking leaves, instead of bending forwards from the waist and twisting, stand with feet apart, pointing forwards. Then shift your weight in a rocking motion, moving forwards and back rhythmically. Use your abs to keep your trunk aligned, ribs over hips.

To rise from a chair, slide forwards to the edge of the seat, right angles at both knees. Then pull your abs in and lean forwards from your hips, with a straight torso. Place one foot behind the other, come onto the ball of the back foot and push yourself up, using strength from your legs.

useful resources

The resources below provide some useful contact details that will help to give you a good start in finding high-quality exercise equipment. You will also find some organizations and websites with general information on health and fitness if you decide you would like to learn more.

general fitness resources

bbc.co.uk/health
www.bbc.co.uk/health/healthy_living/fitness/
Useful general website with features on the benefits of being fit, how to choose the appropriate type of exercise and finding out how much exercise you need to stay healthy.

Fitness Industry Association
Castlewood House
77–91 New Oxford Street
London WC1A 1DG
www.fia.org.uk
Tel: 020 7554 504
A not-for-profit organisation, which promotes the benefits of a healthy lifestyle and represents the health and fitness sector in the UK.

National Register of Personal Trainers
PO Box 3455
Marlow
Bucks SL7 1WG
www.nrpt.co.uk
Tel: 0870 200 6010

A register of over 800 members nationwide that enables you to find a qualified, insured and experienced personal trainer in the UK.

NHS Choices
www.nhs.uk/Pages/homepage.
Offers a postcode-based search option to help you find local sport and fitness services. Also has a link to the online *Live Well* magazine with a wide variety of general health features.

Sport England
3rd Floor Victoria House
Bloomsbury Square
London WC1B 4SE
www.sportengland.org
Tel: 020 7273 1551
The Government agency responsible for advising, investing in and promoting community sport.

The Register of Exercise Professionals of the United Kingdom
8–10 Crown Hill
Croydon
Surrey CR0 1RZ

www.exerciseregister.org
Tel: 020 8686 6464
The register helps safeguard and promote the health and interests of people who use the services of exercise and fitness instructors, teachers and trainers. Offers a search facility.

UK Sport
40 Bernard Street
London WC1N 1ST
www.uksport.gov.uk
Tel: 020 7211 5100
UK Sport works in partnership with Sport England, **sport**scotland, the Sports Council for Wales and the Sports Council for Northern Ireland and other agencies. It coordinates overall UK sport policy, supports elite sport, manages the international relationships of the UK and coordinates a UK-wide approach to international issues. UK Sport is funded by, and responsible to, the Department for Culture, Media and Sport.

YMCA England
640 Forest Road
London E17 3D
www.ymca.org.uk
The largest single voluntary
sector organization offering a
wide range of individual and
group services including exercise
classes and fitness studios that
are accessible and inclusive for
people of all ages and skill levels.
The website has a search facility
to help you find your nearest
YMCA.

where to buy equipment

Fitness Mad
Units 2–4 Willersey
    Industrial Estate
Willersey
Worcs WR12 7RR
Tel: 01386 85955
www.fitness-mad.com
Specializes in products for yoga,
Pilates, core stability, resistance
and strength-training.

Newitt & Co. Ltd.
Claxton Hall
Flaxton
York
North Yorks YO60 7RE
www.newitts.com
Family firm offering sports
equipment by mail order. Supplier
of gym balls and exercise mats.

Sissel UK Ltd.
10 Moderna Business Park
Mytholmroyd
Hebden Bridge
West Yorks HX7 5QQ
www.sisseluk.com

Tel: 01422 885433
For their own-brand cushioned
exercise mats and sports balls of
varying sizes.

Totally Fitness
www.totallyfitness.co.uk
Tel: 0800 056 43
Offers a wide range of gym and
fitness equipment including
medicine balls of various weights.

clothing

sweatyBetty
833 Fulham Road
London, SW6 5HQ
www.sweatybetty.com
Tel: 0800 169 3889
Founded in 1998 by Tamara Hill-
Norton, sweatyBetty sells
gorgeous clothing for active and
not-so-active women in
boutiques nationwide and online.

other books by
Joan Pagano

15-Minute Total Body Workout
(Dorling Kindersley, 2008)
Tone up and get fit with the
combined cardio-strength
training programmes, presented
with easy-to-follow instructions
and a high-quality companion
DVD. The four 15-minute
routines can be learned in the
book and performed along with
the DVD – a realistic time
commitment for busy people on
the go.

8 Weeks to a Younger Body
(Dorling Kindersley, 2007)
Whatever your actual age, you
can beat your body-clock and
drop a decade with these
specially designed exercises.
Find out how to stay young as
you increase your personal
fitness levels and overall health.

Strength Training Deck
(Dorling Kindersley, 2006)
Based on Joan's popular book,
Strength Training for Women, the
exercise-card deck combines
straightforward information with
fresh, clean design in a portable
format of 52 exercises to sculpt
and strengthen the body.

Strength Training for Women
(Dorling Kindersley, 2005)
This step-by-step strength-
training manual features
exercises to help you shape and
tone your body. Joan shows you
how to get the best out of your
workout, improving both your
strength and stamina for long-
lasting results.

to contact
Joan Pagano

Joan Pagano Fitness Group
401 East 89th Street (# 2M)
New York, NY 10128
www.joanpaganofitness.com
email: info@joanpaganofitness.
com

index

acknowledgments

Thank you to all of my family and friends for their patience and encouragement during the long days of writing. To James for his infinite TLC and for keeping me on balance. To my mother for always caring. And to my sister Lucy for coming to my rescue once again.

Thank you to my clients for sharing the path – for years of loyalty, for being supportive and accommodating, and for having a spirit of adventure.

Thank you, DK, for the opportunity to reach out to women around the world and to work with an outstanding team of professionals. To Mary-Clare Jerram and Jenny Latham for steering the project. To my editor, Hilary Mandleberg, for all the ways she enhanced this work and for her determination to ensure the best results. To Ruth Hope for her stunning artistic vision and to Ruth Jenkinson for her brilliant photography. And to Carla and Jacqui, our models, for being so lovely, inside and out.

Publisher's acknowledgments

Dorling Kindersley would like to thank photographer Ruth Jenkinson and her assistant Ann Burke; sweatyBetty for the loan of some of the exercise clothing; Viv Riley at Touch Studios; the models Jacqui Freeman and Carla Collins; Victoria Barnes and Roisin Donaghy for the models' hair and makeup; Anna Toombs and David Robinson of TR Balance for additional training support; Hilary Bird for the index.

All images © Dorling Kindersley.
For further information see www.dkimages.com

about Joan Pagano

Joan Pagano, a Phi Beta Kappa cum laude graduate of Connecticut College, is certified in health and fitness instruction by the American College of Sports Medicine (ACSM), whose credentials provide the very best measure of competence as a professional. She has worked as a personal fitness trainer on Manhattan's Upper East Side in New York since 1988, providing professional guidance and support to people at all levels of fitness. Through her work, she has created hundreds of training programmes for individuals, groups, fitness facilities, schools, hospitals, and corporations. For many years, she served as the Director of Personal Trainer Certification Programme at Marymount Manhattan College.

Today, Joan manages her own staff of trainers in the Joan Pagano Fitness Group. She is a nationally recognized provider of education courses for fitness trainers through IDEA (an organization supporting fitness professionals worldwide) as well as an authority on the benefit of exercise for women's health issues such as pregnancy, breast cancer, menopause, and osteoporosis. She is the author of *15-Minute Total Body Workout, 8 Weeks to a Younger Body, Strength Training Deck*, and *Strength Training for Women*, for which Weight Watchers bought the serial rights.